72 Guiding Lights
Colour In ♦ Meditate ♦ Learn

For a Journey of Self Discovery

Penelope Smith

THE SANGREAL SODALITY PRESS

Johannesburg, Gauteng, South Africa

First edition 2017

Published by The Sangreal Sodality Press
74 Twelfth Street
Parkmore 2196
Gauteng
South Africa
Email: Jacobsang@gmail.com

Copyright © 2017 Penelope Smith

All rights reserved. No part of this publication may be reproduced or transmitted in any form or by any means, be it electronic or mechanical, photocopied, photographed or recorded without the written permission of the Author or publisher.

ISBN 978-0-620-76156-7

Contents

INTRODUCTION 1

WAYS IN WHICH TO ENJOY THIS BOOK 3

HOW TO PREPARE YOURSELF 4

COLOURING IN SECTION 5

LEARNING SECTION 151

    THE 72 GUIDING LIGHTS 153

    HOUSES 154

    ZODIAC SIGNS 155

    PLANETS 156

    ENERGY OF COLOURS 157

    THE 72 GUIDING LIGHTS POSITIONED AROUND THE ASTROLOGY WHEEL 158

    SAMPLE OF NATAL (BIRTH) CHART WHEEL, SHOWING PLANETS AND DEGREE 159

    SAMPLE OF PERSONAL CHART WITH THE GUIDING LIGHTS AROUND 160

WORKSHEET SECTION 161

    TEMPLATE FOR YOUR BIRTH CHART MATRIX 163

    WHEEL OF GUIDING LIGHTS TEMPLATE 165

    CREATE YOUR OWN AMULET 167

    AMULET TEMPLATE 169

APPENDIX A 171

    LIST OF GUIDING LIGHTS 171

BIBLIOGRAPHY 175

Introduction

This is a book designed for a fun, relaxing, healing and learning experience by using the meditative process of colouring in. Colouring in enables you to awaken your higher levels of consciousness and find a deeper understanding of yourself. This process makes use of Astrology, your Guiding Lights, and Mandalas. These are Universal Systems, which reveal your gifts, allowing you to understand and tune into your purpose.

Why Meditate? To look within. Meditation relaxes and stills the mind to reach a state of altered consciousness. Meditating helps clear the mind to enhance focus while untangling your energy field. It tunes your vibration to be more receptive to the universal teachings. Meditation is about listening and observing the world around you for answers that you may be seeking.

Why colour in? To connect with inner Self. It has the power to enhance creativity, imagination and can help with healing. A relaxed mind does not create challenges.

Why circle art or Mandalas? A circle has no beginning or end, symbolic of you at the centre point extending yourself outwards in all directions. Mandalas represent the cosmos and finding your way through life, giving you the ability to stretch your energy to the extents of the Universe.

Why Astrology? A tool. The Stars inspired man from his early existence. Before lights and TV, man gazed at up at the night skies and studied the Stars, as they were a constant in his life. Noticing that events happened when the Stars were in certain places, the ancients learned to document those correlations and a picture emerged leading to Astrology. These concepts have become a practical science for us to discover our purpose. Astrology links Heaven, our Minds and Souls in the dance of life through time. Your Astrological Birth Chart is a picture of the Heavens, at the time you took your first breath, showing the positions of the Zodiac Signs and Planets, in relation to where you were born. A Birth chart is the blueprint of your life's story with all its potentials and possibilities. How you tell and create your story is up you. The University of Life is there to teach and guide us.

Why Guiding Lights? To Learn from. The Lights are our source of energy, inspiration, guidance and protection. Meditation and colouring in are ways to connect with these Lights to absorb their knowledge. They are the link to our higher consciousness and known by many other names such as Spirit Lights, Guardian Angels, Genii of the Spheres and the 72 fold names of Destiny. I believe Einstein, Newton, Leonardo da Vinci and other great thinkers were able to automatically link into or meditated on these Lights resulting in their genius.

When born into the Physical World, our brain is a mass of neural pathways wide open to the wisdom of the 72. Children have imaginary friends teaching them. These friends are the 72 Lights they have externalized. As we go through life, we form more connections relevant to surviving in a physical form and through the stresses and strains of everyday life, lose these connections and pathways. As a result, the 72 fade, we forget about our "Source" and start to rely on external help and guidance.

This book is a resource to help you reconnect with your Guiding Lights. The colouring in process reconnects those lost pathways to awaken new ideas, self-confidence, good health and many other attributes.

Everyone will have his or her own unique experience, whilst meditating and colouring in. Some may feel a rush of energy, a feeling of opening up and see a new brightness in the world around, whilst others may feel nothing or have feelings of foreboding. The universe will only allow you to experience that which you can cope with. One person will find this experience as enjoyable and another unsettling. Another important lesson is that something perceived as bad happening is not necessarily bad. It may be the best thing for you, as it could take your life in a completely new direction affording you new opportunities and life lessons. There is no such thing as good or bad. All clouds have a silver lining; our job is to find the gift in the lining. There are no guarantees of success as everyone's idea of advancing and finding their ideals is different.

Pick up your colouring pencils, crayons, chalks, whatever your chosen medium and start colouring your way towards an Enlightened Soul, utilising these unseen powers who are there to direct the way.

Penelope Smith

Durban

Ways in which to enjoy this book

1) Just enjoy a moment in your own space with your own thoughts.

2) Use as a calendar.

   a) Place the book on your desk or hang it on a wall, open at the Light you wish to enjoy. This will connect you to their energies each day.

3) Bring out the deeper thoughts of life:

   a) Find the Light that rules over your birthday, the Light that has been with you all the time. Through this book, you can become aware of the Lights power in your life and acknowledge this energy.
   Example: your birthday is 4 April; your Light would be Sit.
   Find your Light by looking through the dates on the list of Lights in Appendix A

   b) Learn the names of the Six Guiding Lights that rule over your birth sign. Recite them as a mantra in meditation, for protection or healing or before going to sleep if you have a question in mind in order to wake up with an answer.
   Example: Aries six Lights are, Vehu, Yeli, Sit, Elem, Mahash, Lelah. Find the six Lights that rule your birth sign in Appendix A.

   c) Find your own personal Lights. These lights are linked to the positions of the planets in your birth chart at the time of your birth. There are ten planets in astrology so you could have up to ten Lights to guide over the aspect of your life they represent. Most will find they have a few less than ten as some guiding lights rule over two or more planets. You will find your lights by linking the planets in your chart to the relevant 72. This is explained in more detail in the working section.

   d) With these names, you can create a personalized amulet.
   A template design with instructions to create your own amulet can be found in the workbook section.

How to prepare yourself

On opening your book, chose your purpose. Are you looking for a playful fun experience, have a particular purpose in mind, or in search of some deeper insights to life. Focus on a question or a challenge you are trying to solve or just want to have a quiet time to reflect and see where your mind goes.

Find a quiet space in a relaxed atmosphere, still your mind and say a few words like:-

I acknowledge the presence of the Guiding Lights,
Guide and protect me during my meditation,
Using the power within me,
I open my heart and mind to welcome your intelligence.
So shall it be.

As you start colouring, take a few deep breaths, slow your energy down and focus on what you seek. Give respect and acknowledgement to your higher self and the higher powers.

Relax your mind, as you go deeper into a relaxed state. Feel the connections with the energies opening to bring out of yourself the knowledge that is hidden deep within and enjoy the moment.

When you are finish colouring in, sit for a while and relax in the moment. Become one with the energies around you then slowly start to come back to the present and become aware of your surroundings.

Say some closing words such as:-

Thank you for your direction, your guidance and protection,
allow me to free my mind,
so that I may take all I have discovered to new places to grow and guide others.
So shall it be.

Spend a moment in contemplation and put any thoughts you have down in your journal. Stretch and go for a short walk.

Colouring in Section

This section is for you to set your spirit free, allow your imagination to grow wings and start your journey to become one with the 72 Lights.

"Angels are the interface through which a man interacts with the awesome Light of the Creator. However, our senses of perception are, by design, restricted and limited. Consequently, the force called "angel" remains unobservable to the naked eye and illogical to the rational mind. Like the unseen wind, however, it's influence is very real. Positive actions of sharing, tolerance & compassion ignite positive angels. Selfishness intolerance & hatred rouse negative angels."

The Zohar

Let your spirit fly, high high into the Sky
Let your imagination free, deep deep into eternity.
Let your soul go, way way beyond the world we know.

1 - Vehu

Spiritual Guiding Light of 0° - 4° Aries
21 March - 25 March
Energy for strength, motivation and leadership.

2 - Yeli

Spiritual Guiding Light for 5° - 9° of Aries
26 March -   30 March
Energy for positive decision making.

3 - Sit

Spiritual Guiding Light for 10° - 14° of Aries
31 March - 4 April
Energy for stimulating new ideas and action.

4 - Elem
Spiritual Guiding Light for 15° - 19° of Aries
5 April - 9 April
Energy to heighten awareness and confidence.

מהש

5 - Mahash
Spiritual Guiding Light for 20° - 24° of Aries
10 April - 14 April
Energy for learning, and easy transitions and change.

6 - Lelah

Spiritual Guiding Light for 25° - 30° of Aries
15 April - 20 April
Energy for healing and balancing mind, body and spirit.

אכא

7 - Acha

Spiritual Guiding Light 0° - 4° Taurus
21 April - 25 April
Energy for patience and focus.

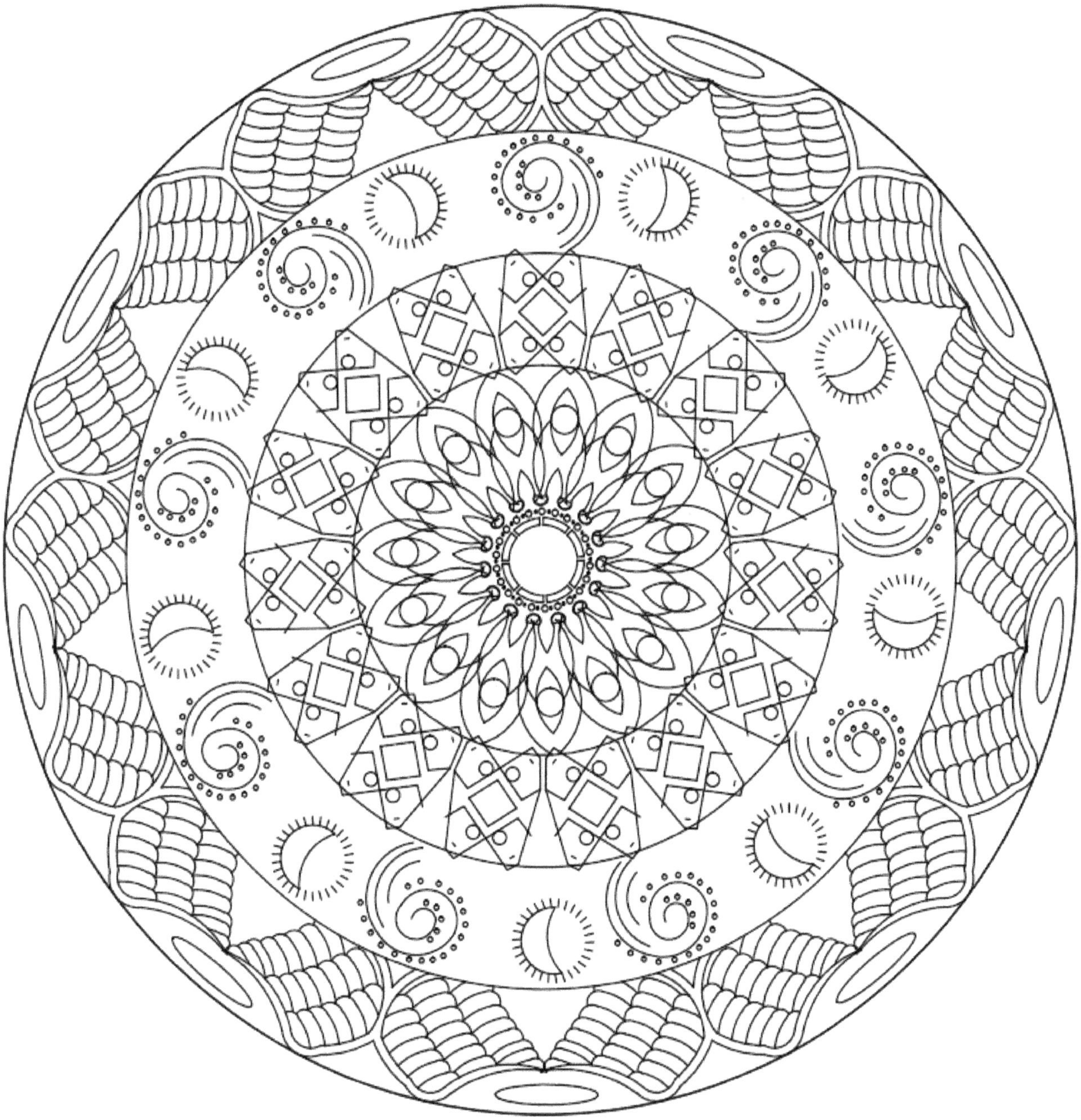

כהת

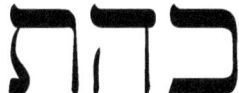

8 - Kahet

Spiritual Guiding Light for 5° - 9° of Taurus

26 April - 30 April

Energy for removing negative energies.

9 - Hezi

Spiritual Guiding Light for 10° - 14° of Taurus
1 May - 5 May
Energy of Mercy and Forgiveness.

10 - Elad
Spiritual Guiding Light for 15° - 19° of Taurus
6 May - 10 May
Energy for Protection from physical attacks.

לאו

11 - Lav

Spiritual Guiding Light for 20° - 24° of Taurus
11 May - 15 May
Energy for Victory over failure and lessons learned.

12 - Haha

Spiritual Guiding Light for 25° - 30° of Taurus
16 May - 20 May
Energy for self-value and completions of tasks.

13 - Yezel

Spiritual Guiding Light 0° - 4° Gemini
21 May - 25 May
Energy for forming Alliances.

14 - Mebah

Spiritual Guiding Light for 5° - 9° of Gemini
26 May - 31 May
Energy for Truth, Liberty and Justice.

15 - Hari

Spiritual Guiding Light for 10° - 14° of Gemini
1 June - 5 June
Energy to bring out creative and artistic abilities.

16 - Hakem

Spiritual Guiding Light for 15° - 19° of Gemini.
6 June - 10 June.
Energy for dealing with depressions and adaptability.

17 - Lav

Spiritual Guiding Light for 20° - 24° of Gemini.
11 June - 16 June
Energy for focus when writing.

18 - Keli

Spiritual Guiding Light for 25° - 30° of Gemini
17 June - 21 June
Energy for Justice so the innocent can triumph.

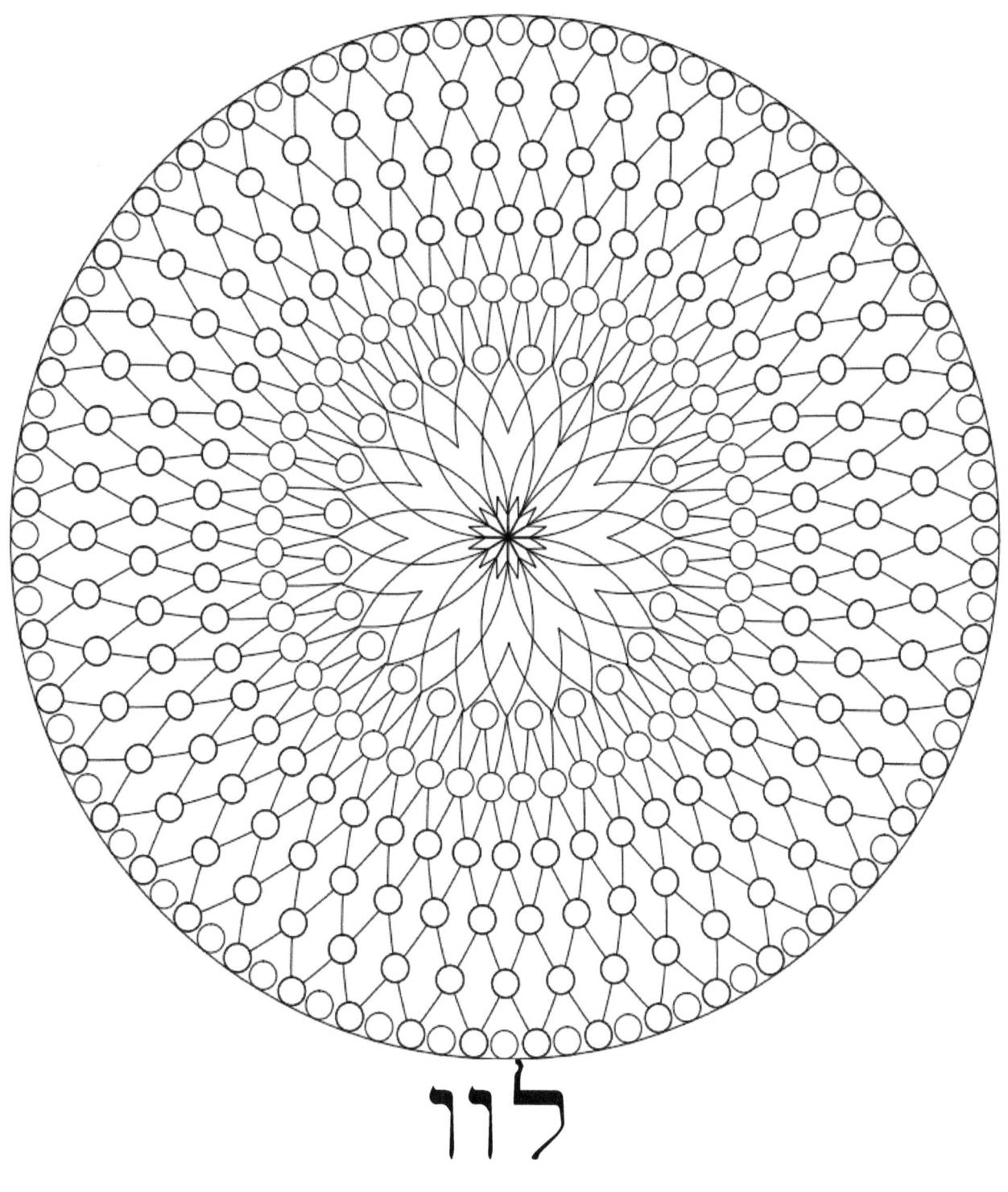

19 - Lov

Spiritual Guiding Light 0° - 4° Cancer
22 June - 26 June
Energy for Empathy and to stimulate the sixth sense.

20 - Pahal

Spiritual Guiding Light for 5° - 9° of Cancer
27 June - 1 July
Energy for financial independence and choosing partners.

21 - Nelach

Spiritual Guiding Light for 10° - 14° of Cancer
2 July - 6 July
Energy for the destruction of evil.

22 - Yeyay
Spiritual Guiding Light for 15° - 19° of Cancer
7 July - 11 July
Energy for overcoming past pains for future wellness.

23 - Melah

Spiritual Guiding Light for 20° - 24° of Cancer
12 July - 16 July
Energy for Healing and growing healing Plants.

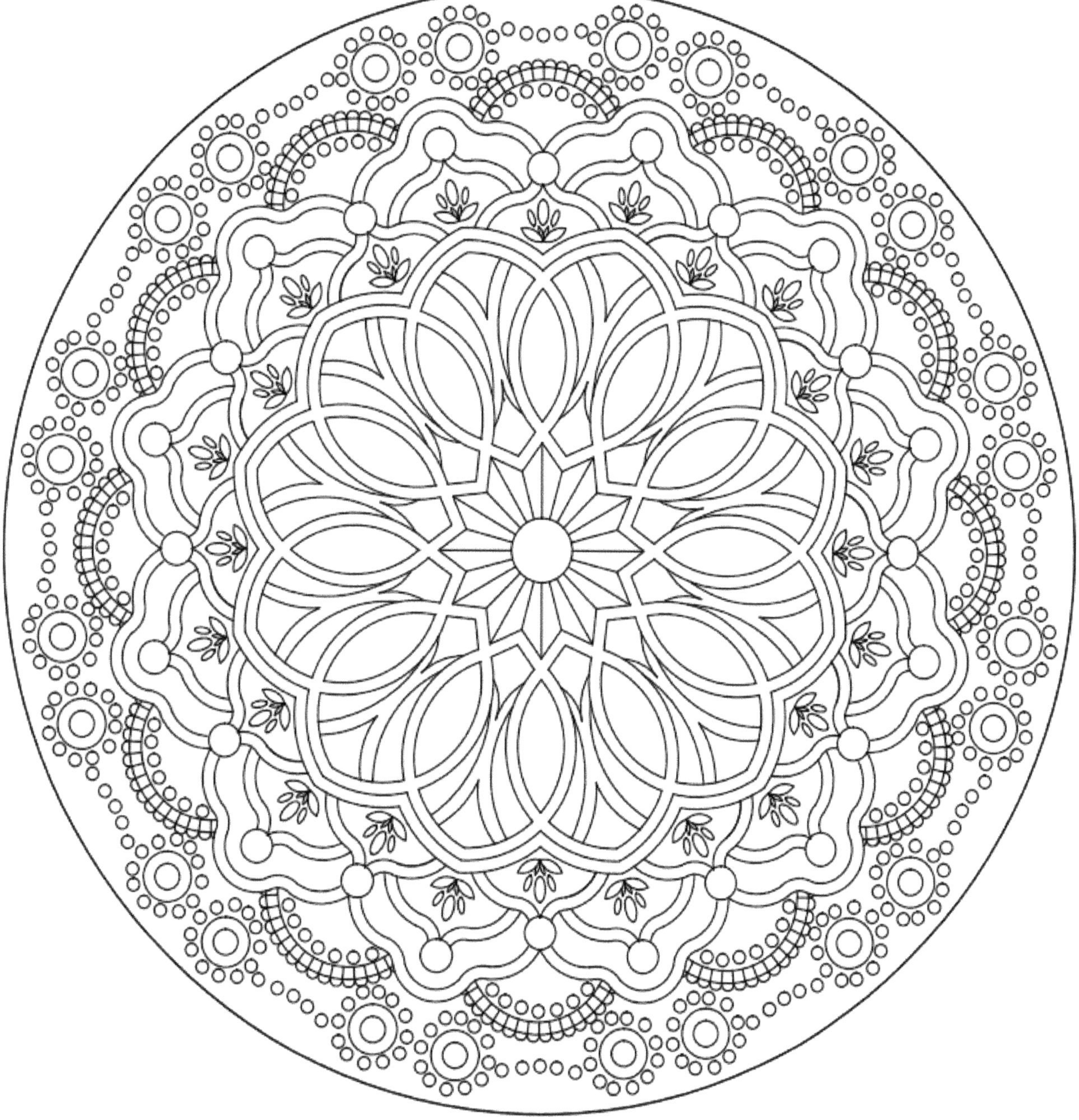

חהו

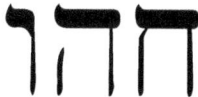

24 - Chaho

Spiritual Guiding Light for 25° - 30° of Cancer

17 July - 22 July

Energy for emotional, mental wellness and freedom.

נתה

25 - Netah

Spiritual Guiding Light 0° - 4° Leo
23 July - 27 July
Energy for answers and to eliminate fear.

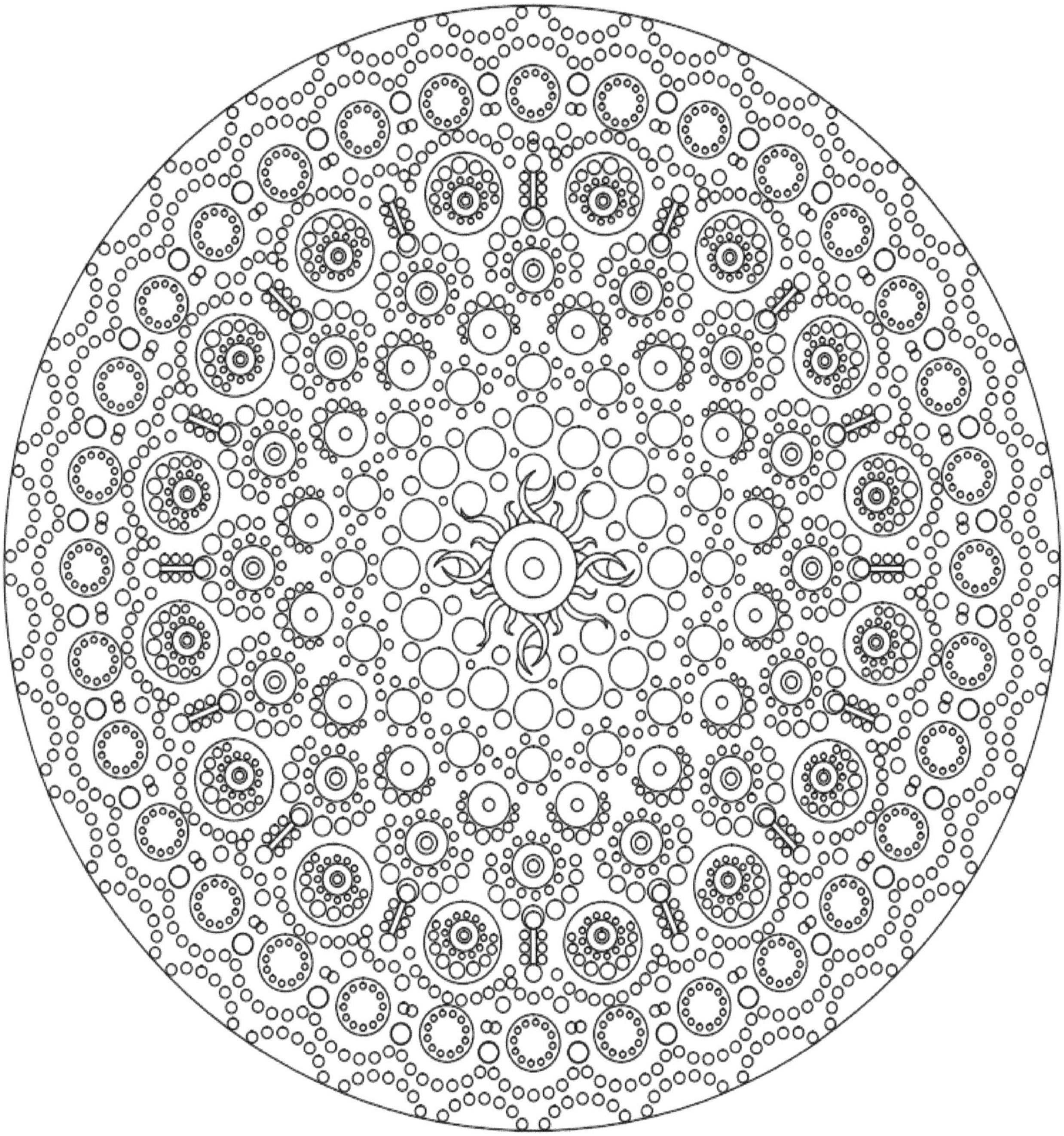

26 - Ha'a

Spiritual Guiding Light for 5° - 9° of Leo
28 July - 1 August
Energy for giving and receiving respect.

ירת

27 Yeret

Spiritual Guiding Light for 10° - 14° of Leo
2 August - 6 August.
Energy of Abundance.

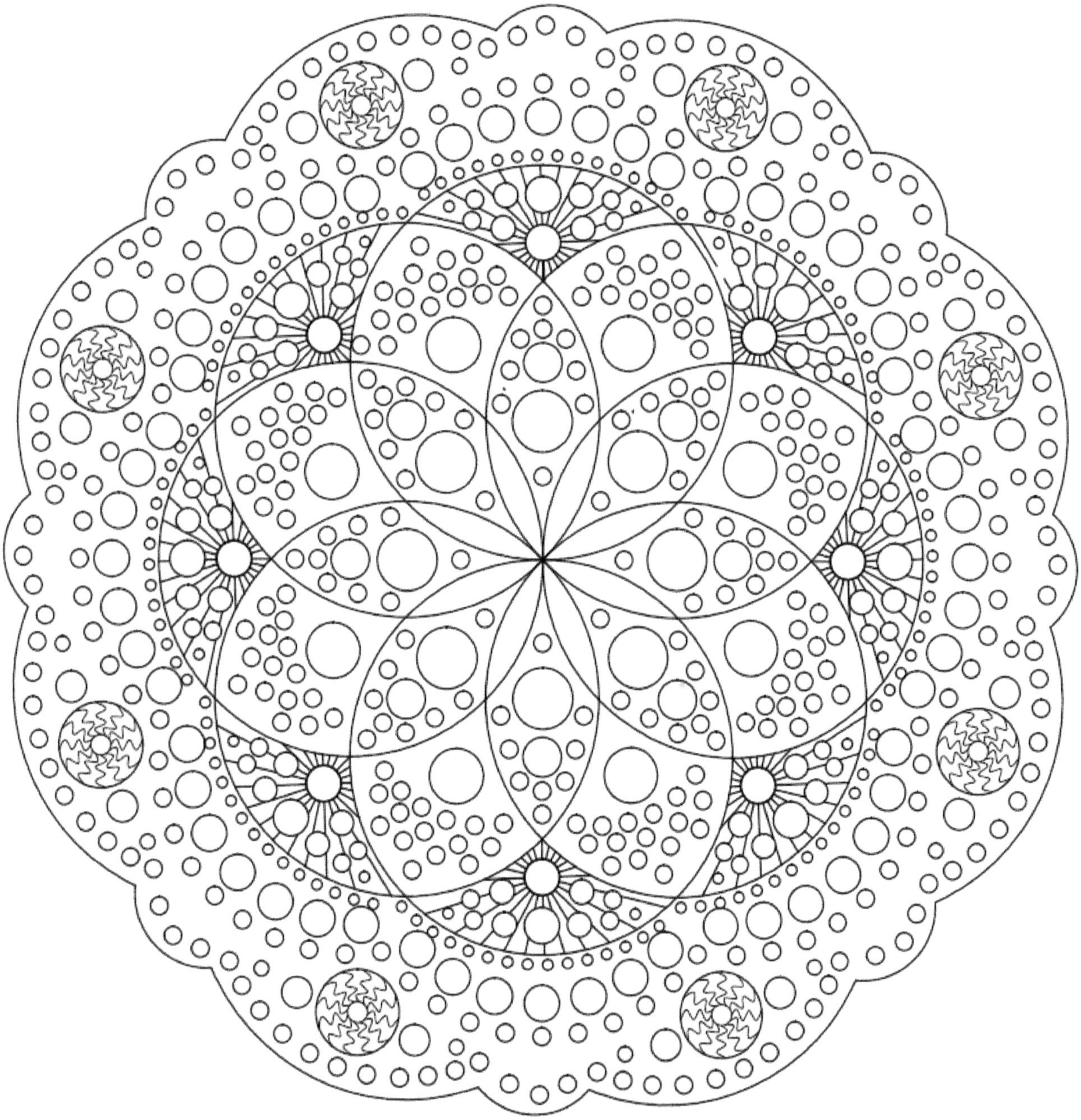

שאה

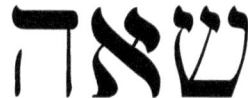

28 Sha'ah

Spiritual Guiding Light for 15° - 19° of Leo
7 August - 14 August
Energy for Longevity.

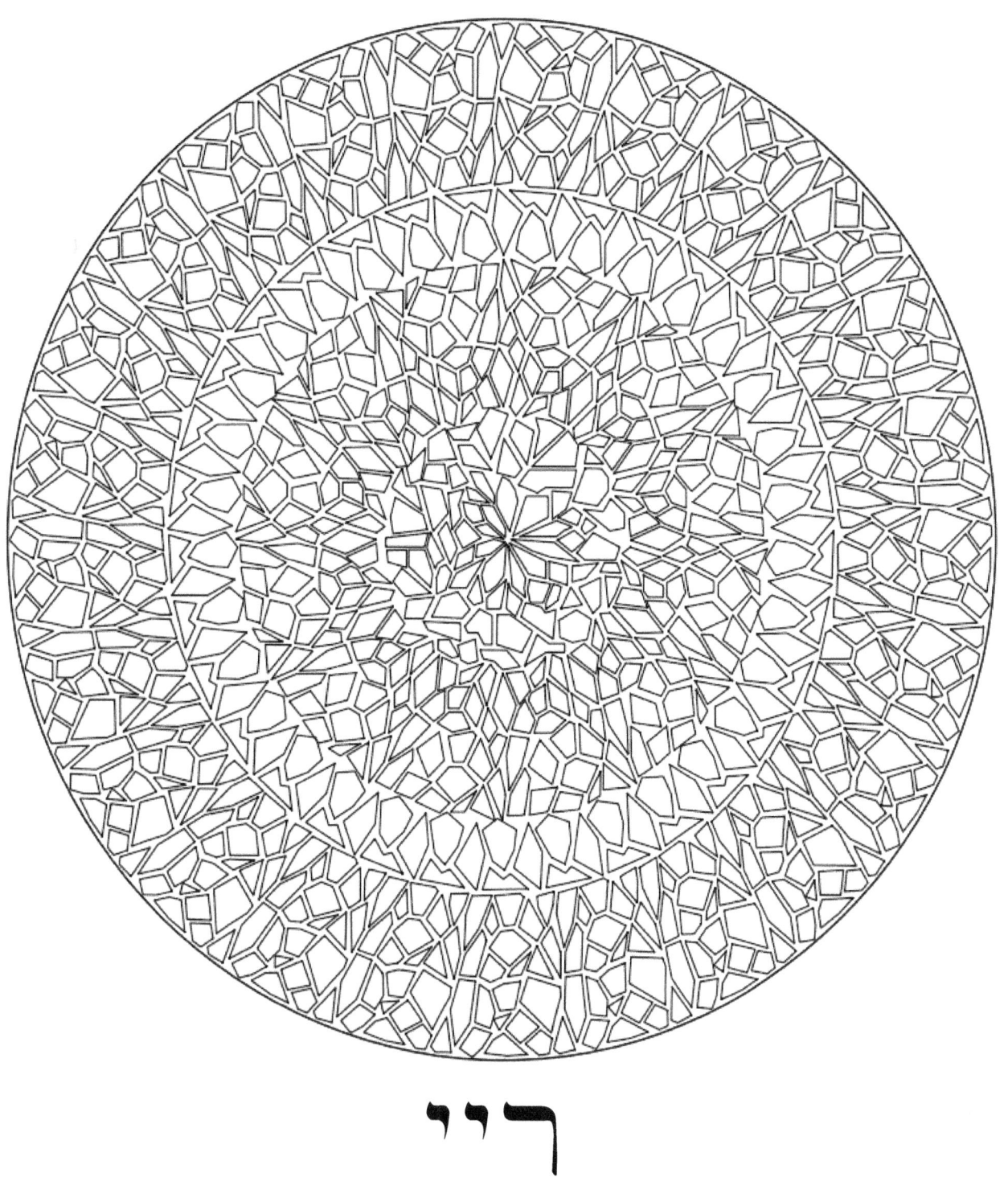

29 Riyi

Spiritual Guiding Light for 20° - 24° of Leo
13 August - 17 August
Energy for Liberation from Hatred.

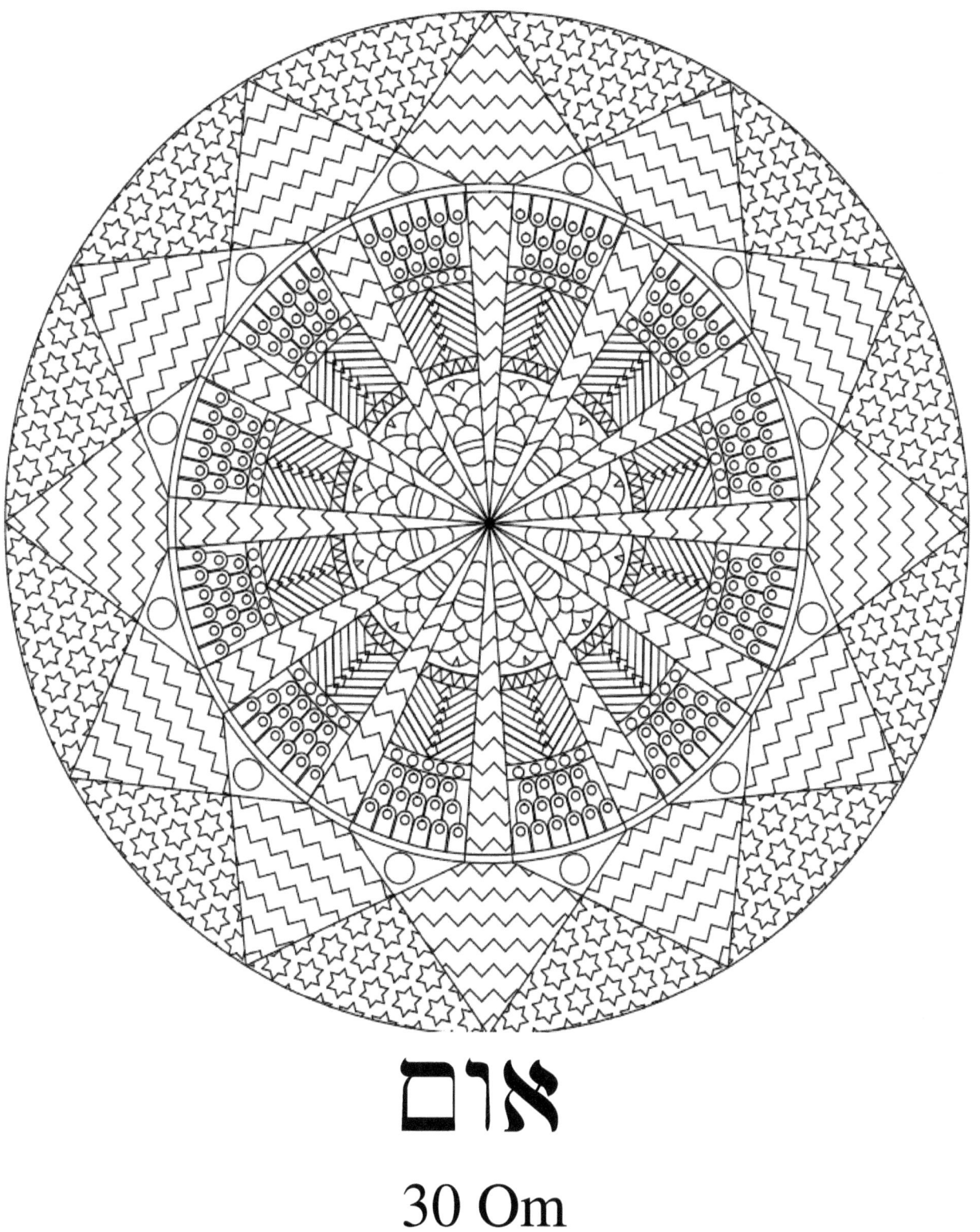

אום

30 Om

Spiritual Guiding Light for 25° - 30° of Leo
18 August - 22 August
Energy for Bridge Building to higher understanding and risk taking.

31 - Lekav

Spiritual Guiding Light 0° - 4° Virgo
23 August - 28 August
Energy for overcoming obstacles to finish projects.

32 - Vesher

Spiritual Guiding Light for 5° - 9° of Virgo
29 August - 2 September
Energy for breaking old cycle of repeated mistakes and learn the lesson.

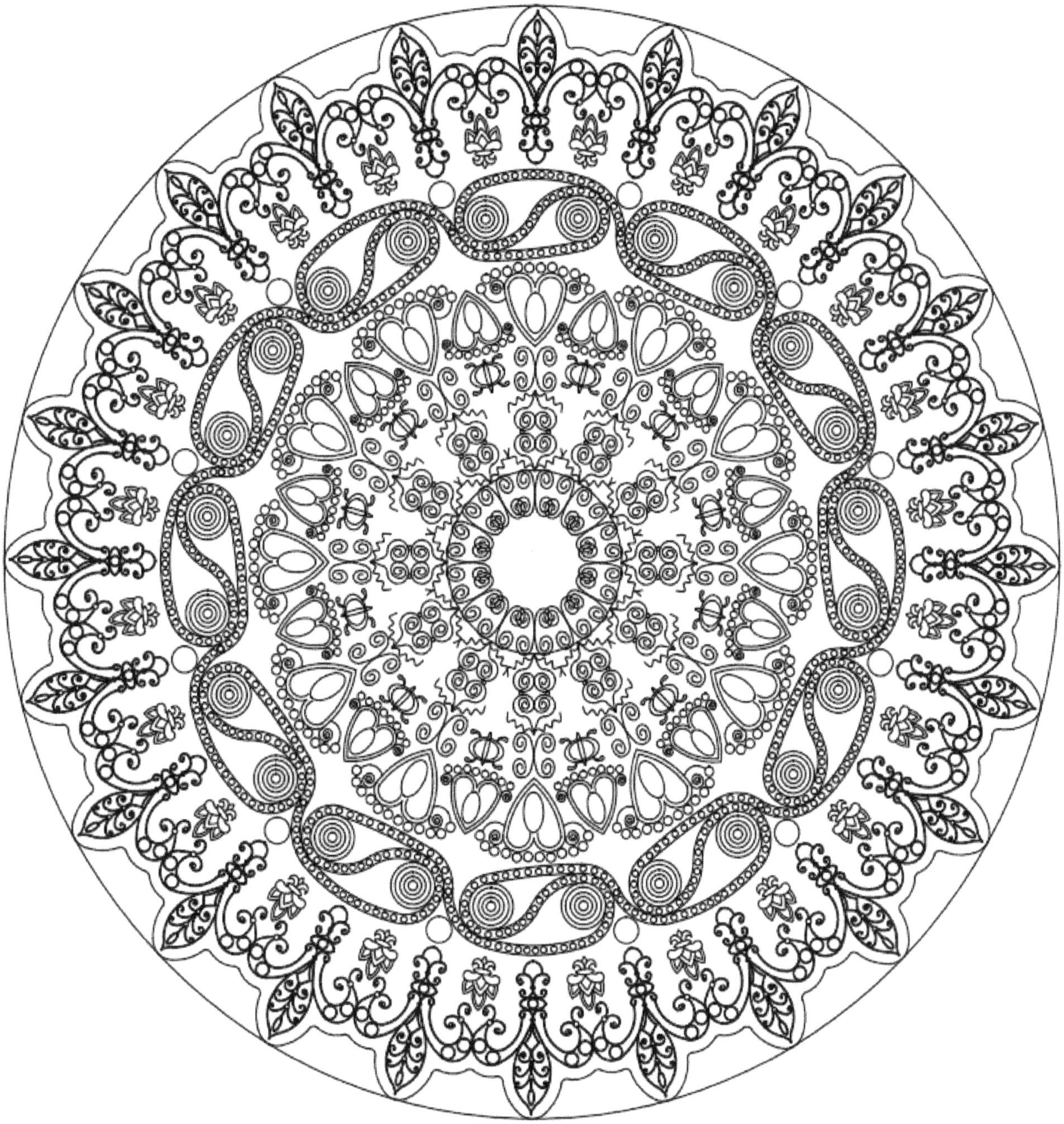

יחו

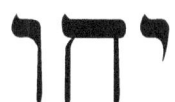

33 - Yichu

Spiritual Guiding Light for 10° - 14° of Virgo
3 September - 7 September
Energy for comfort in times of sorrow.

34 - L'hach

Spiritual Guiding Light for 15° - 19° of Virgo
8 September - 12 September
Energy for confidence and finding the perfectionist within.

כוק

35 - Kevek

Spiritual Guiding Light for 20° - 24° of Virgo
13 September - 17 September
Energy for amicable Legal matters.

מנד

36 - Menad

Spiritual Guiding Light for 25° - 30° of Virgo
18 September - 23 September
Energy for inner and outer strength

37 - Ani

Spiritual Guiding Light 0° - 4° Libra
24 September - 28 September
Energy for seeing the big picture.

חעם

38 - Cha'am
Spiritual Guiding Light for 5° - 9° of Libra
29 September - 3 October
Energy for Ritual and Ceremonies.

רהע

39 - Reho
Spiritual Guiding Light for 10° - 14° of Libra
4 October - 8 October
Energy for balance and harmony.

40 - Yeyiz

Spiritual Guiding Light for 15° - 19° of Libra
9 October - 13 October
Energy for choosing the right words to transform reality.

41 - Hahah

Spiritual Guiding Light for 20° - 24° of Libra
14 October - 18 October
Energy for balance of feelings.

מיך

42 - Mich

Spiritual Guiding Light for 25° - 30° of Libra
19 October - 23 October
Energy for protection from conspiracies set to destroy.

43 - Veval

Spiritual Guiding Light 0° - 4° Scorpio
24 October - 28 October
Energy for spiritual evolution.

44 - Yelah

Spiritual Guiding Light for 5° - 9° of Scorpio
29 October - 2 November
Energy for creating a better self and world.

45 - Se'al

Spiritual Guiding Light for 10° - 14° of Scorpio
3 November - 7 November
Energy for harmony with nature and overcome jealousy.

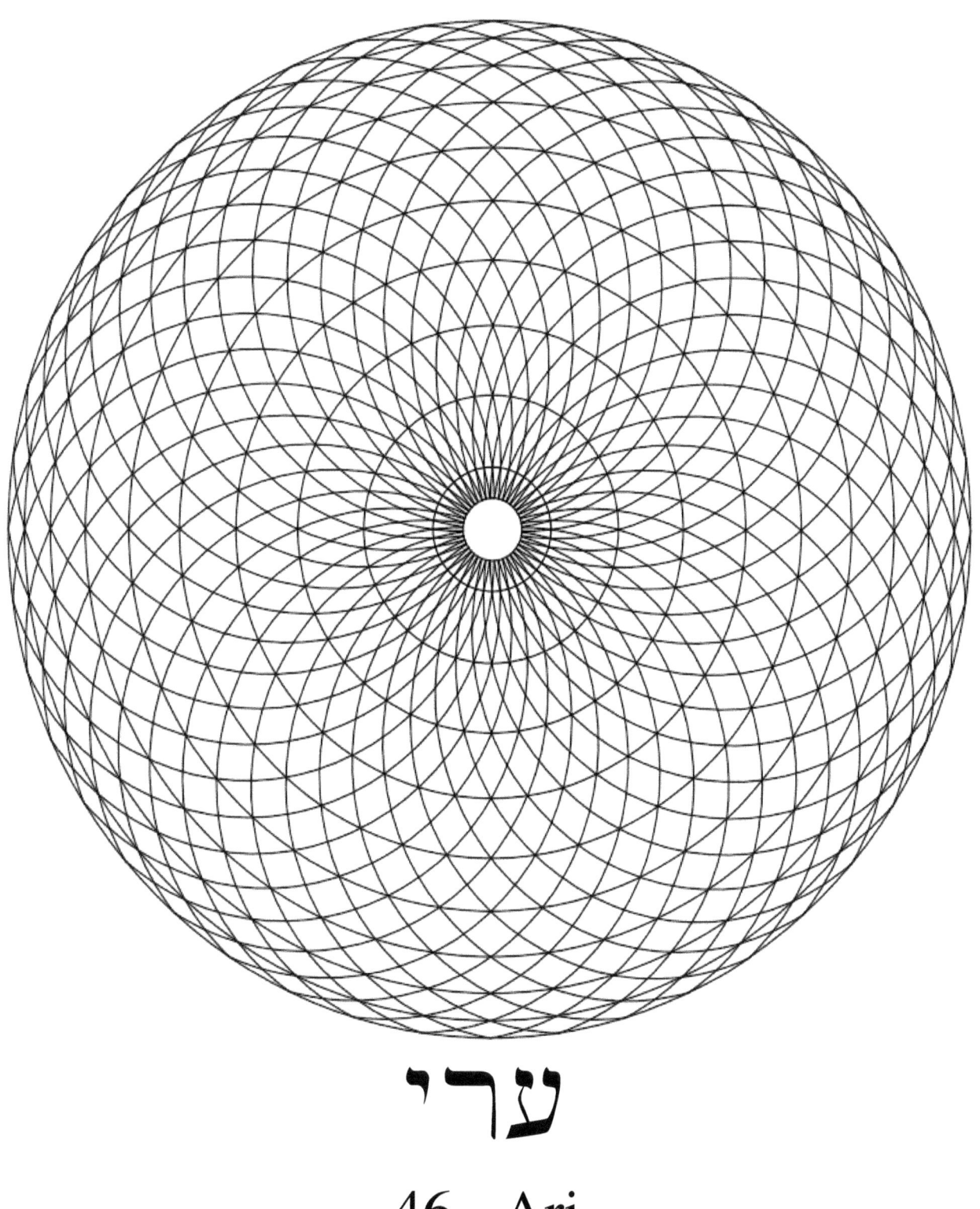

46 - Ari

Spiritual Guiding Light for 15° - 19° of Scorpio
8 November - 12 November
Energy for revealing the secrets nature holds.

47 - Eshal

Spiritual Guiding Light for 20° - 24° of Scorpio
13 November - 17 November
Energy for contemplation.

מיה

48 - Mih

Spiritual Guiding Light for 25° - 30° of Scorpio
18 November - 22 November
Energy for working together in relationships and discovering your worth.

49 - Vehu

Spiritual Guiding Light 0° - 4° Sagittarius
23 November - 27 November
Energy that gives your soul what it needs not what your ego wants.

50 - Dani

Spiritual Guiding Light for 5° - 9° of Sagittarius
28 November - 2 December
Energy for awakening and developing soul growth.

51 - Hachash

Spiritual Guiding Light for 10° - 14° of Sagittarius
3 December - 7 December
Energy for giving and receiving forgiveness.

52 - Omem

Spiritual Guiding Light for 15° - 19° of Sagittarius
8 December - 12 December
Energy for connecting to a higher understanding and working with the light.

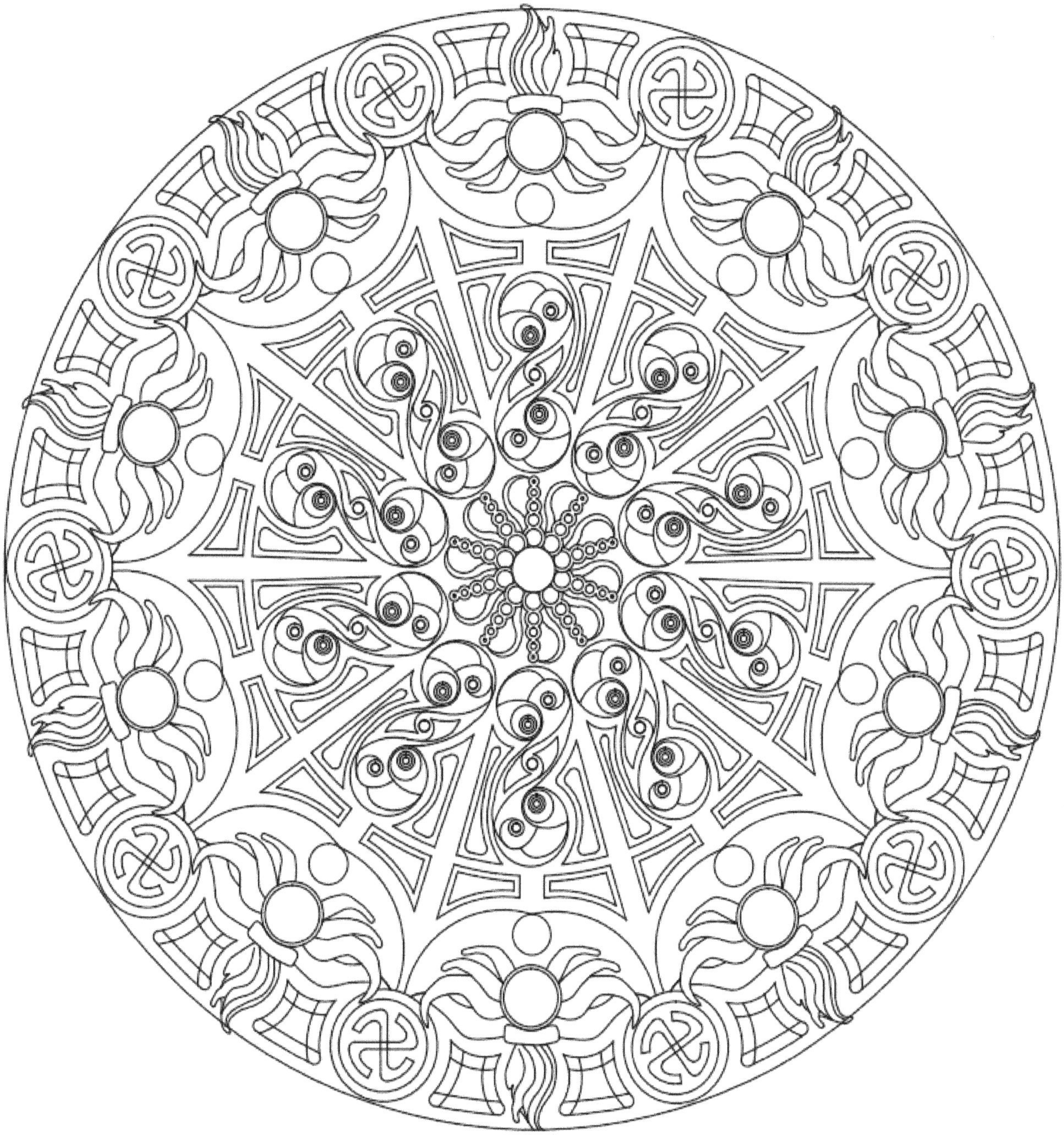

ננא

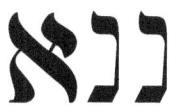

53 - Nena

Spiritual Guiding Light for 20° - 24° of Sagittarius
13 December - 16 December
Energy for Loving Kindness.

נִית

54 - Nit

Spiritual Guiding Light for 25° - 30° of Sagittarius
17 December - 21 December
Energy for the elixir of life, passion for it and self-transformation.

55 - Mivah

Spiritual Guiding Light 0° - 4° Capricorn
22 December - 26 December
Energy for entering the world of dreams.

56 - Poi

Spiritual Guiding Light for 5° - 9° of Capricorn
27 December - 31 December
Energy for unblocking your full potential.

57 - Nemem

Spiritual Guiding Light for 10° - 14° of Capricorn
1 January - 5 January
Energy for removing limitations to bring prosperity in all things.

58 - Yeyil
Spiritual Guiding Light for 15° - 19° of Capricorn
6 January - 10 January
Energy for healing physical ailments.

59 - Harach

Spiritual Guiding Light for 20° - 24° of Capricorn
11 January - 15 January
Energy for intellectual richness.

מצר

60 - Metzer

Spiritual Guiding Light for 25° - 30° of Capricorn
16 January - 20 January
Energy for solving challenges.

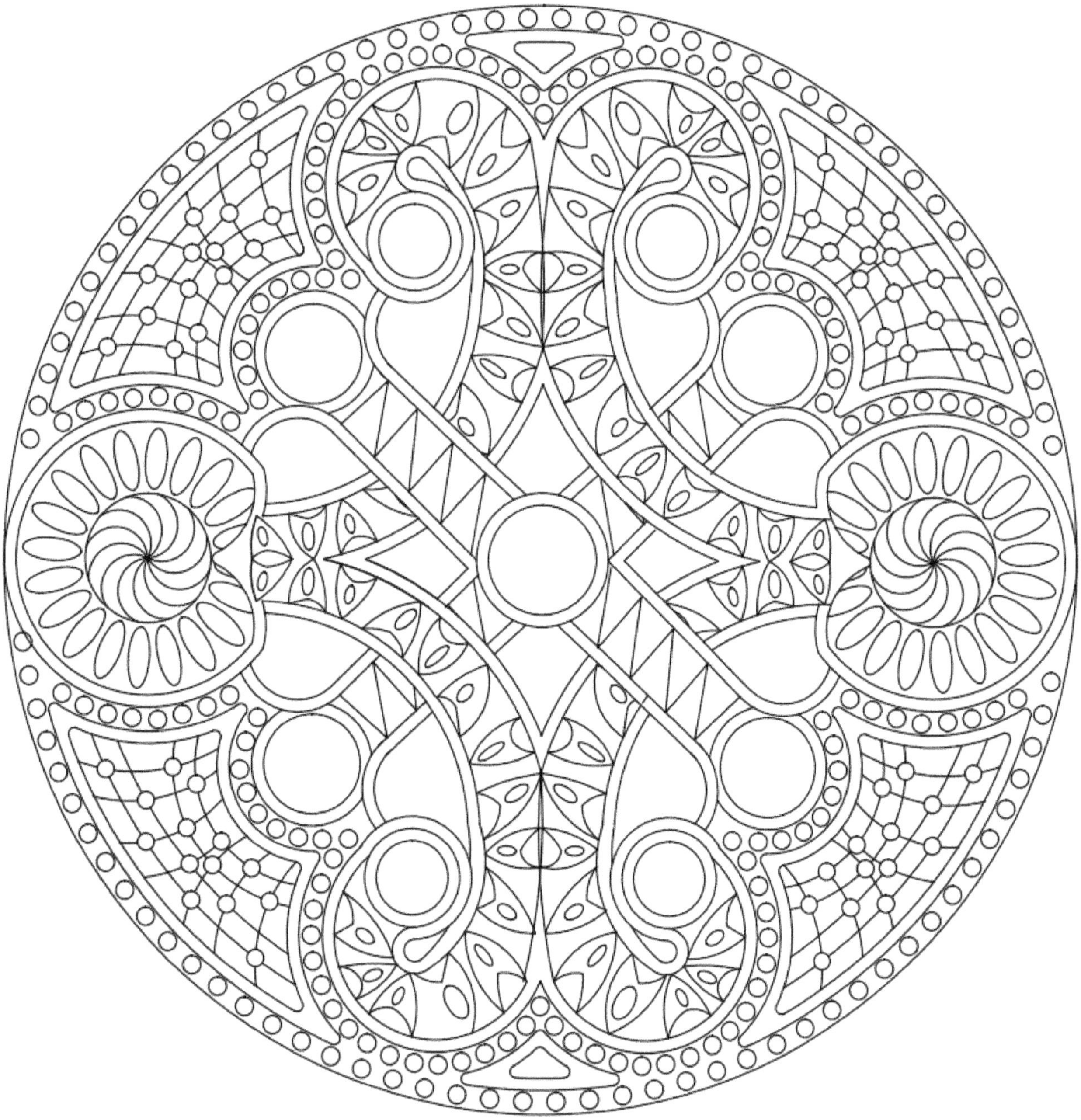

ומב

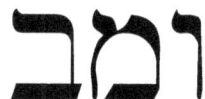

61 - Umab

Spiritual Guiding Light 0° - 4° Aquarius
21 January - 25 January
Energy for independent forward thinking.

62 - Yahah

Spiritual Guiding Light for 5° - 9° of Aquarius
26 January - 30 January
Energy for courage to live through your own truth.

63 - Anu

Spiritual Guiding Light for 10° - 14° of Aquarius
31 January - 4 February
Energy for respect for all the diversity in the world

64 - Machi

Spiritual Guiding Light for 15° - 19° of Aquarius
5 February - 9 February
Energy for creating great success and gathering information.

65 - Dameb

Spiritual Guiding Light for 20° - 24° of Aquarius
10 February - 14 February
Energy for connecting with the fountain of wisdom.

מנק

66 - Menak

Spiritual Guiding Light for 25° - 30° of Aquarius
15 February - 19 February
Energy for calming down anger.

אי ע

67 - Iya
Spiritual Guiding Light 0° - 4° Pisces
20 February - 24 February
Energy for overcoming disappointment and creating something better.

חבו

68 - Chavu
Spiritual Guiding Light for 5° - 9° of Pisces
25 February - 29 February
Energy of healing Emotional issues and stopping repetitive bad habits.

ראה

69 - Ra'ah

Spiritual Guiding Light for 10° - 14° of Pisces
1 March - 5 March
Energy for finding lost and stolen property.

70 - Yabam

Spiritual Guiding Light for 15° - 19° of Pisces
6 March - 10 March
Energy for removing blockages in the soul.

71 - Hayi

Spiritual Guiding Light for 20° - 24° of Pisces
11 March - 15 March
Energy for transforming consciousness.

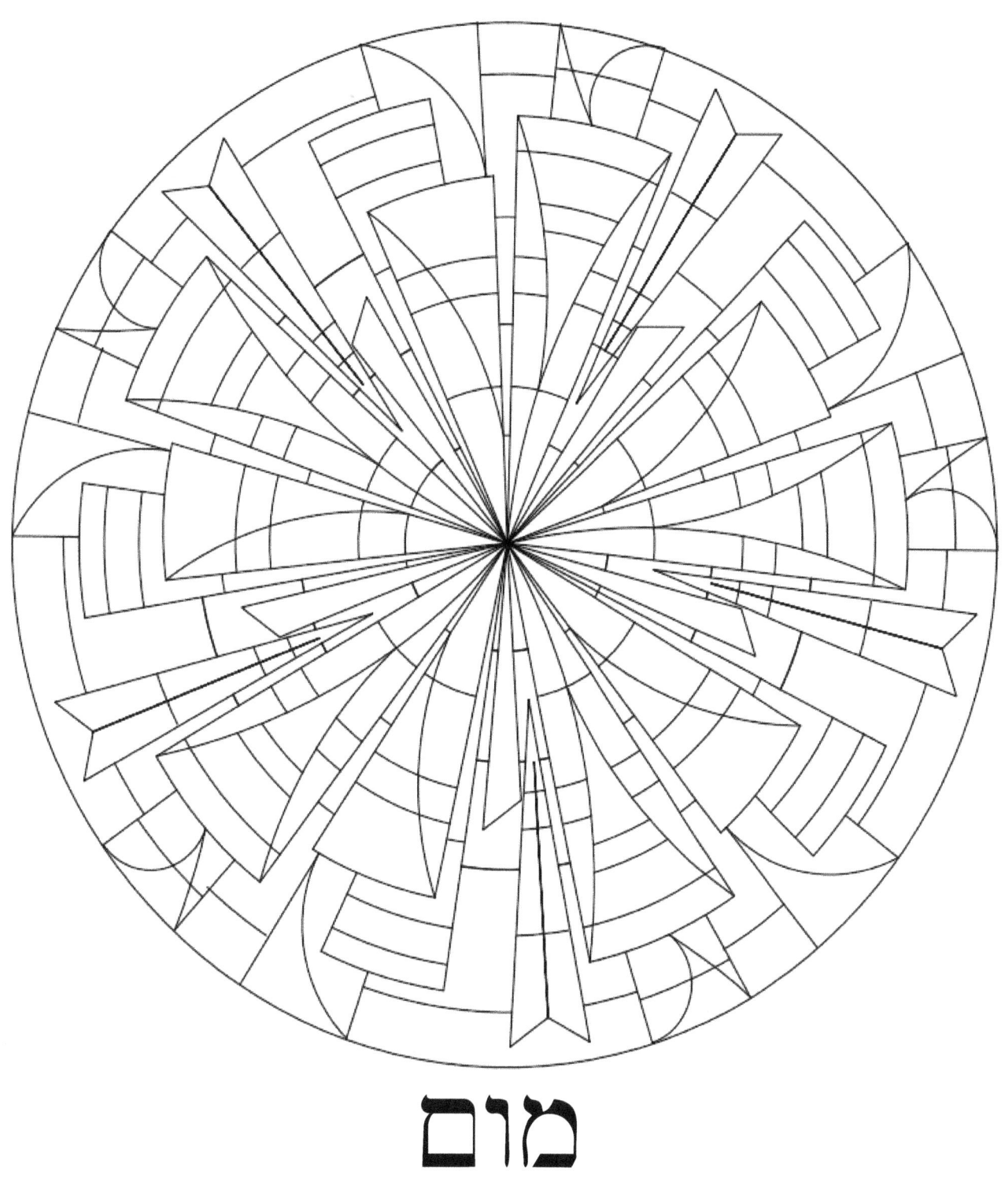

מום

72 - Mum

Spiritual Guiding Light for 25° - 30° of Pisces
16 March - 20 March
Energy for spiritual cleansing for the next cycle and new beginnings.

Learning Section

This section will introduce you to, and outline the thoughts and energies behind, the 72 Guiding Lights, Astrological Houses, Zodiac signs, Planets and Colours.

Included are diagrams showing you where the Lights are positioned around the Astrology Wheel and how to match them up to your own birth chart to achieve this.

Set your mind free, way way beyond reality.
Set your desire on fire, free free to inspire.
Set your dreams alight, go go ignite.

The 72 Guiding Lights

The concept of the 72 Guiding Lights comes from Sacred Texts and Kabbalistic writings that set out the various attributes a Creator of the Universe would have. The detail behind the Lights is a vast subject on its own. Fortunately, we are able to extract the essence of the writings and thoughts in order to use them in various ways. Colouring in is one of these ways to help you tune your vibration into the energies of the 72, to absorb and utilise their knowledge.

Everything in creation has a vibration with a frequency and pitch. These frequencies and pitches create movement and movement creates sound and rhythm.

Words and thoughts have their own rhythm; we use our vocal cords to form sounds creating a vibration. Because of their vibration, words carry the power of intent. They can heal, motivate, cheer, calm, inspire and energise. Putting words together in poetry and song make us feel alive, happy, depressed, and draw on memories from songs, which connect generations. Anything that stimulates the brain, a picture, a smell, will create a rhythm. Psychics and sensitive people are able to translate the messages within the rhythm, into words we understand.

Being one with creation, we each have a unique rhythm or name of our own within the rhythm/name of creation. Our rhythm is the power of the universe at work on an individual basis within each of us. We have our attributes, strengths and weaknesses. Each of the 72 has an attribute that is there for us to draw from. We absorb the knowledge they contain by tuning our energy into that of the Lights.

The 72 mandalas for colouring in have been designed so that one may learn each of their names and become familiar with their energy in order to start the tuning in process.

To work with the energies unique to our purpose and align our vibrations with our individual sets of Lights, we turn to Astrology in search of our signature. You will discover how to do this in the learning section at the back of the book.

The path to understanding yourself is a personal journey.

Enjoy discovering.

Houses

Astrology charts have 12 Houses, representing you and your environment; 1-6 represent self-matters. 7-12 represent outside interests. House positions on the wheel never move, like the numbers around a clock. Signs and Planets move like the hands of the clock.

1	(Self)	Body, vitality, personality, appearance, energy. How we observe the world, present ourselves and begin things.
2	(Personal Possessions)	Money, material goods, values, hidden talents. How we obtain, use and replenish our resources.
3	(Communications)	Thinking, talking, writing stills, early education, ability to absorb information. How we communicate with the world.
4	(Home)	Home, family, parents, land or family estates. How we create a home and develop ourselves.
5	(Creative Self-expression)	Children, fun, risks taking, creative skills, sport. How we express ourselves creatively.
6	(Work & Health)	Health, daily duties, work, service. How we will serve self and others.
7	(Relationships)	Partnership in marriage, business, close friendships and the way we relate to others, agreements and legal matters. How we set the ground rules in relationships.
8	(Endings & New Beginnings)	Deep down issues, inheritances, partners, other people's money, death, sex, taxes, debt. How we relate to the death and birth of everything
9	(Higher Leaning)	Growth in views, beliefs, searching for meaning and truth,. How we challenge our minds.
10	(Career)	Profession, ambition, long-term goals, reputation, status, contribution to life. How we aim for what we want.
11	(Friendships and Groups)	Friends, groups, rewards, hopes, dreams and thoughts about the world How we plan our lives to obtain what we dream of.
12	(Retreats & institutions)	Represents hidden issues, retreats, hospitals, retirement, secrets, How we understand the cycles of life.

Zodiac Signs

The Zodiac is made up of 12 Signs that circle the sun in an annual cycle. Each sign has its own traits and talents and its own strengths and weakness.

Aries ♈ (Challenger) Purpose: To inspire others with great ideas. Objective is to establish own identity and focus on self.

Taurus ♉ (Path Finder) Purpose: To bring value and meaning to the world. Objective feel one with nature and express the beauty of its soul.

Gemini ♊ (Inspirer) Purpose: To create balance in relationships. Objective is mindfulness; learn to focus on one idea until completion.

Cancer ♋ (Career) Purpose: To provide stability, security and comfort. Objective, to balance emotion and express your creativity.

Leo ♌ (Conductor) Purpose: To shine bright and lead the way. Objective, to balance giving and receiving.

Virgo ♍ (Analyst) Purpose: To serve and heal others. Objective, learn how to give criticism constructively.

Libra ♎ (Mediator) Purpose: To find the middle path. Objective, to create balance & harmony in own life and not delay making decisions.

Scorpio ♏ (Transformer) Purpose: To play devil's advocate in search of truth. Objective, to learn to help other, take responsibility, and listen to your gut instincts.

Sagittarius ♐ (Advisor) Purpose: To teach a broader perspective to life. Objective, to focus on the positive, learning as you go.

Capricorn ♑ (Disciplinarian) Purpose: To teach higher ideals. Objective is self-understanding and it is ok to lead the way in following rules.

Aquarius ♒ (Idealist) Purpose: To pass knowledge gained on to others. Objective is self-understanding and

Pisces ♓ (Seeker) Purpose: To lead the way into the next realm. Objective, not to let fear of failure hold them back.

Planets

The Planets represent the leader and his advisors, tasked to oversee challenges indicated by their position in your chart. They have a mutual commitment to make sure you have the best experience this life can offer you. The planets placement in your own chart, will determine where their energies will manifest and where you will shine, grow and learn in this life.

Sun ☉ (The Leader)   I am   Energy, dignity, self-expression.
Your Sun's Guiding Light enhances vitality, strengthen your character

Moon ☽ (Moral Counsel)   I Feel   Emotional, instincts, prudence.
Your Moon's Guiding Light enhances ability to reflect and absorb love.

Mercury ☿ (The Author)   I Think   Enquiring mind, logic, speaking stills.
Your Mercury' Guiding Light enhances free-minded thinking and the rapid comprehension of facts.

Venus ♀ (The Judge)   I Enrich   Passions, affections, co-operation.
Your Venus Guiding Light can enhance spiritual, material balance and the pursuit of a common purpose.

Mars ♂ (The General)   I Act   Driving force, action, initiative, desire.
Your Mars Guiding Light can enhance your driving force and help you pursue new ideas, make new discoveries and have great adventures.

Jupiter ♃ (The Developer)   I Enlarge   Joy, luck, success, morals.
Your Jupiter Guiding Light can enhance the desire to grow and improve self.

Saturn ♄ (The Teacher)   I Achieve   Restrictions, hard work, strict justice.
Your Saturn Guiding Light can enhance ability to grab opportunities that come your way and to find your real worth.

Uranus ♅ (The Architect)   I Transform   Originality, inspiration, change.
Your Uranus Guiding Light can help enhance your intellectual powers and common sense.

Neptune ♆ (The Magician)   I Dream   Desires, ideals, imagination.
Your Neptune Guiding Light can enhance your awareness, peace and success.

Pluto ♇ (The Philosopher)   I Empower   Observation and transformation.
Your Pluto Guiding Light can enhance you powers to excel at new beginning and understand the past.

Energy of Colours

Colour has power and vibrations that make you feel up or down, active or lazy etc. The colours you chose, while meditating on the Guiding Lights, will enhance your experience giving it meaning and power. As you use the colours, feel what they represent within you.

Although colour can represent a personal story, the attributes usually associated with colours are listed here:-

Black   (I challenge life)   Colour of unity and grounding.

Represents: Power, elegance, combined another colours can strengthen that colour.

Red   (I am Desire)   Colour of love and conflict, vibrant with life.

Represents: Strength, passion, energy, vitality, attraction of love, promotes courage and power.

Orange   (I am Creative)   Colour of warmth, abundance of vital energy and creativity.

Represents: Courage, confidence, ambition, and adventure, promotes success.

Yellow   (I am Intuitive)   Colour of bright, happy energy and personal power.

Represents: Optimism, creativity, intellect, clarity of thought.

Green   (I am Successful)   Colour of growth, renewal and connect lower self to higher self.

Represents: Money, fertility, freshness, peace growth.

Blue   (I am Loving)   Colour of communication, truth and honesty.

Represents: Loyalty, trust, intelligence, wisdom knowledge.

Indigo   (I am all seeing)   Colour of the inner mind, universal consciousness and visions.

Represents: Luxury, devotion, wisdom, justice, fairness impartiality.

Violet   (I am all knowing)   Colour of intuition, inspiration.

Represents: Imagination, ambition, inner strength and dreams.

Gold   (I am regal)   Colour of self-confidence, associated with understanding.

Represents: Enlightenment, wisdom, intuitiveness, prosperity.

Silver   (I am spirit)   Colour of truth and understanding,

Represents: Intuition, imagination and inspiration.

White   (I am pure)   Colour of goodness, prosperity, mind, spirit.

Represents: Purity, unity, transcendent, innocence, truth, protection.

The 72 Guiding lights positioned around the astrology wheel

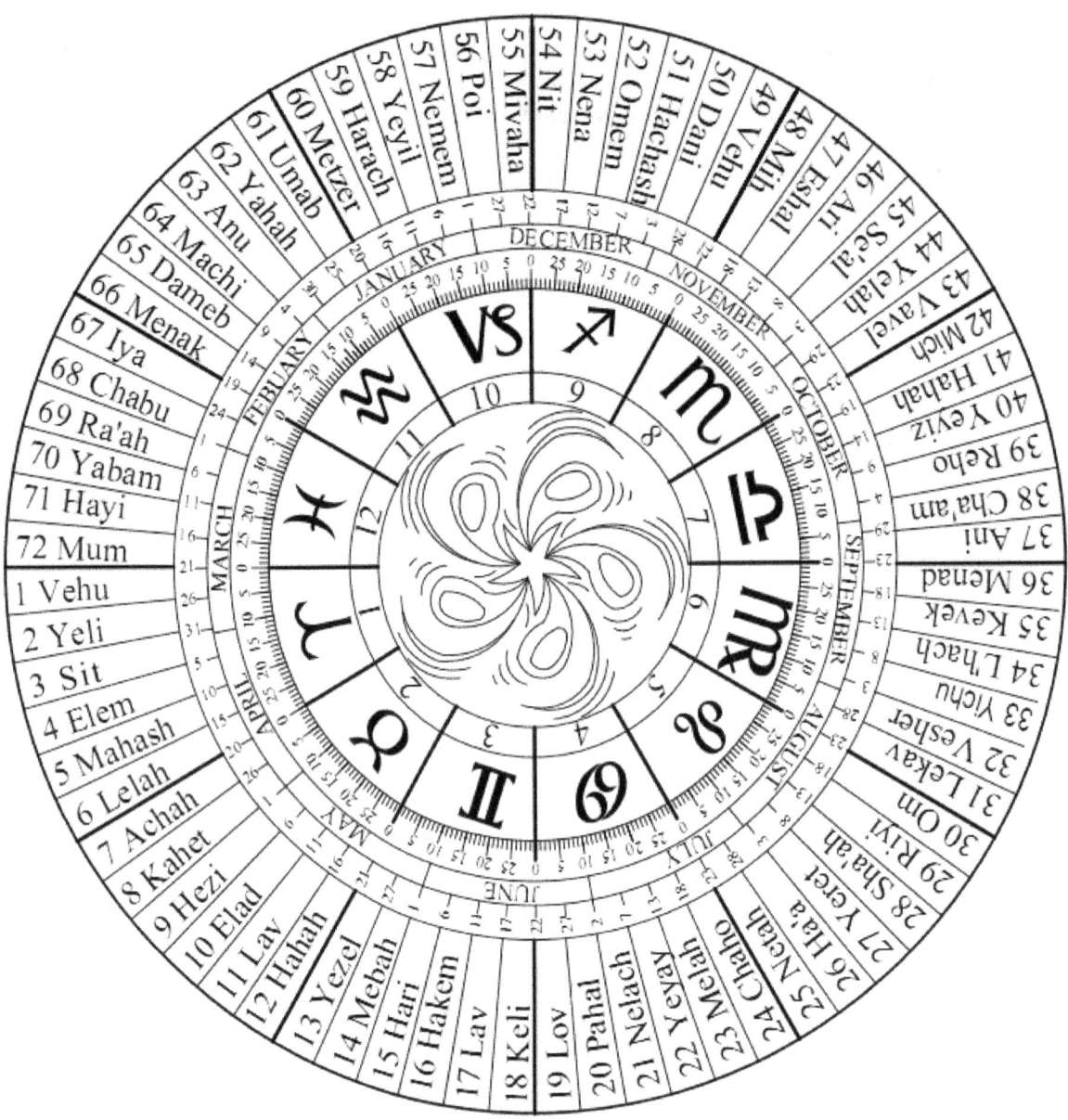

Legend:-

Centre	You, the centre of your universe.
1st circle	The Houses 1 - 12 (fixed in place)
2ne circle	The 12 Sun Signs (in a constant motion around the wheel)
3th circle	Degrees = 30 degrees to each sign = 360 in a full circle.
4th circle	Months
5th circle	Dates
Outer circle	Names of the 72 Guiding Lights

Sample of Natal (birth) Chart Wheel, showing planets and degree

Legend:-

Centre	Owner of chart at the centre of their universe.
1 st circle	House numbers
2nd circle	Planet and Degree Positions (captured at time of birth)
3rd circle	Degrees, 30 degrees to each Sign 360 degrees to a full circle
4th circle	Zodiac Signs (position captured at time of birth).

Example chart: Person born 4 April 1953 in the Northern Hemispheres at 11:20.
Notice that the Sun is at 14° Aries, positioned in the 10th house.
To find the Guiding Light, go to Appendix A, look down for 14° Aries, see that Sit is the Guiding Light of this sun sign. There is a work section at back of book to capture positions of all your planets in your own chart for easy reference.

Sample of personal chart with the Guiding Lights around

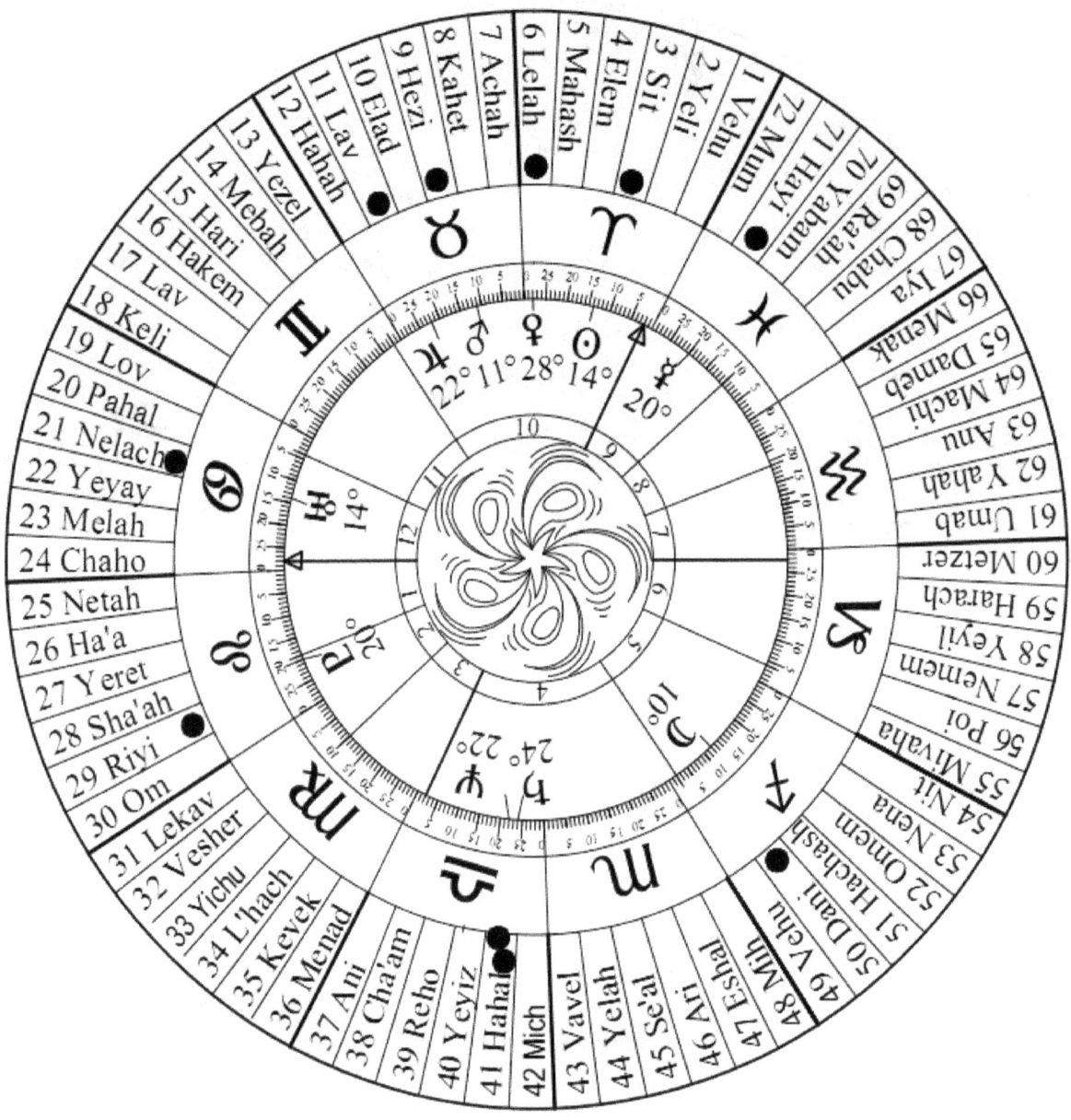

Legend:-

Centre	Owner of chart at the centre of their universe.
1 st circle	House numbers
2nd circle	Planet and Degree Positions (captured at time of birth)
3rd circle	Degrees, 30 degrees to each Sign 360 degrees to a full circle
4th circle	Zodiac Signs (position captured at time of birth).
5th circle	Guiding Lights (in relationship to this personal chart)

A ● indicates the personal Lights in this persons chart. The position of the personal Lights will indicate points in the year, where this person will have extra energy, insights and inspiration.

Worksheet Section

This section includes a Birth chart matrix for you to fill in your planets degrees and signs they sit in, the houses they rule and the Guiding Lights for easy reference.

Included is a template of the Guiding Lights in a circle so that you can position a copy of your own birth chart in the middle. By lining up your Sun sign degree with its relevant Light, you will notice all your other planets will line up to their relevant Light.

There is also a template design to create your own personal Amulet.

Have fun.

Let your heart roar, sing sing feel it soar
Let your feelings go, far far feel the flow
Let your being shine, bright bright into the light

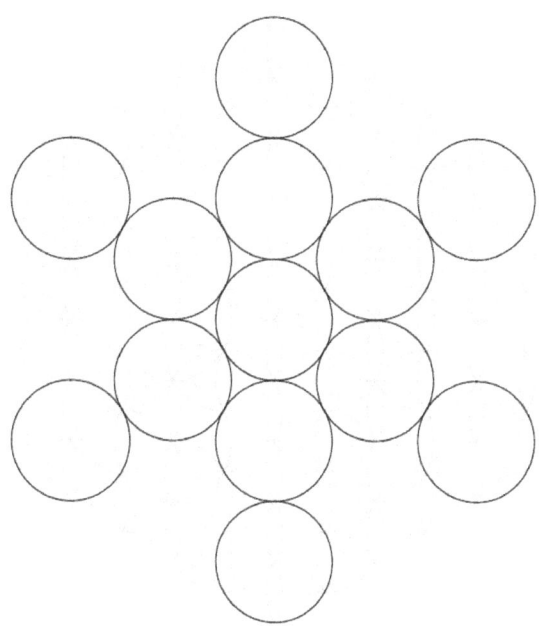

Template for Your Birth Chart Matrix

Your Name		Date of birth	
Time of birth		Place of birth	

Planet	symbol	Sign	Degree	House	Guiding Light	Name
Sun	☉					
Moon	☽					
Mercury	☿					
Venus	♀					
Mars	♂					
Jupiter	♃					
Saturn	♄					
Uranus	♅					
Neptune	♆					
Pluto	♇					

Example from Sample chart

Planet	symbol	Sign	Degree	House	Guiding Light	Name
Sun	☉	♈	14°	10	Sit	סי״ט
The Leader		Challenger		Career	Energy for new ideas and action	

Wheel of Guiding Lights Template

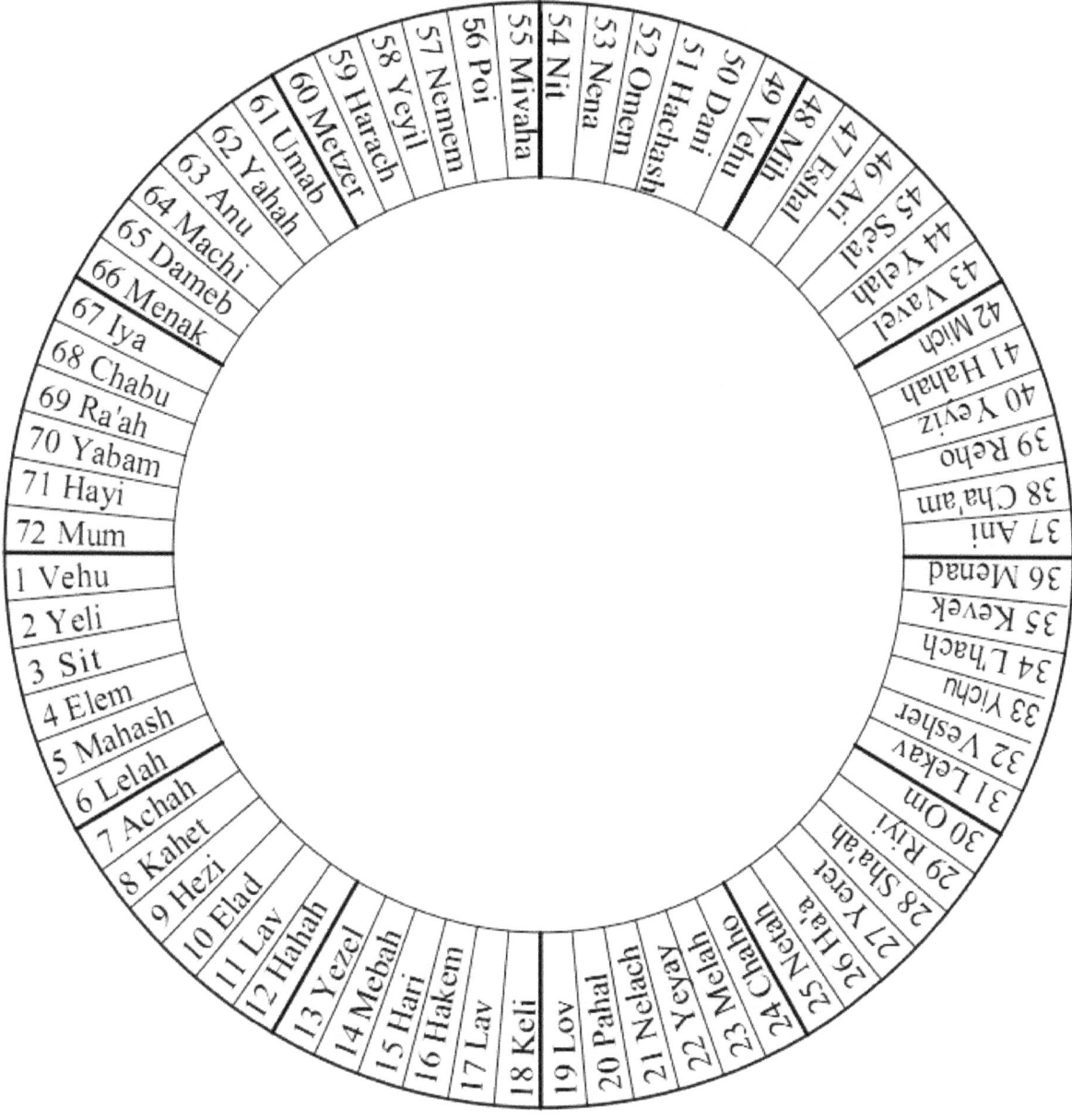

Get a copy of your birth chart. Adjust its size to fit into the middle of the Lights Template. When you have found the Guiding Light that rules over your Sun planet, align your Birth Chart Sun to it, and this will reveal the positions of your other nine lights. You could have ten different Guiding Lights or you may only have three or four, depending on where your planets are positioned.

We all have 10 planets, not all of us will have 10 different Guiding Lights ruling our planets. You may have one Guiding light ruling over a couple or more of your planets. This means that the energies related to the Light you need to lean in more than one aspect of your life.

Create your own Amulet

We live in a world of ritual.

There are rituals for marriages, initiations, rites of passage in all faiths and we surround ourselves every day with symbols and ornaments for love, success and protection.

Amulet are ornaments worn or displayed to attract good luck, good fortune, success, happiness and protection such as wedding bands symbol of unity and love, a badge, a cross. Whether it is a piece of jewellery, a tattoo or an object, it is created with protection or success in mind.

As discussed, we can create an amulet by discovering and using our own unique set of Guiding Lights. The following explains how to achieve this.

To make a power Amulet.

a. Obtain your own birth chart. You can go to an astrologer or download an app off the internet. Either way you will need to supply your name, date, time and place of birth for a chart to be created.
b. Find the position of all the planets in your chart, by their degrees and sign place this info in the birth chart matrix provided in this section then match them with the relevant Guiding Lights and signs they fall under, list found in Appendix A.
c. Take the names of the Guiding Lights and place them around the Amulet template found in this section. Match with the relevant Planet.
d. You can also use the Hebrew symbols to make a beautiful ornament of power. Even if you do not understand Hebrew just looking at the letters will enable you to connect and absorb the energy of the divine name
e. Once you have written the Names or Hebrew letters around the template or put in both, meditate on it, hold it, feel the energy and make it yours.

Ideas to make use of your power object.

a) Use modem technology, take a picture and display as your phone, tablet or computers wallpaper.
b) Place on your desk in a nice frame and refer to it, from time to time, repeating the names.
c) Make a medallion; put on a chain around your neck, the medallion will operate like a Stargaze, taking the energies associated with the Lights to keep you tuned in to the Universe.
d) Embed the image in your mind, to print itself on your third eye. Learn the name's from 1 to 10 starting at the top. If there are two names the same, repeat those names so that you still end up with ten. Create a musical line using the names to make them easier to remember. In times of stress or meditation, repeat the names using your Lights names in song and call on your Guiding Lights to help you out.

Amulet Template

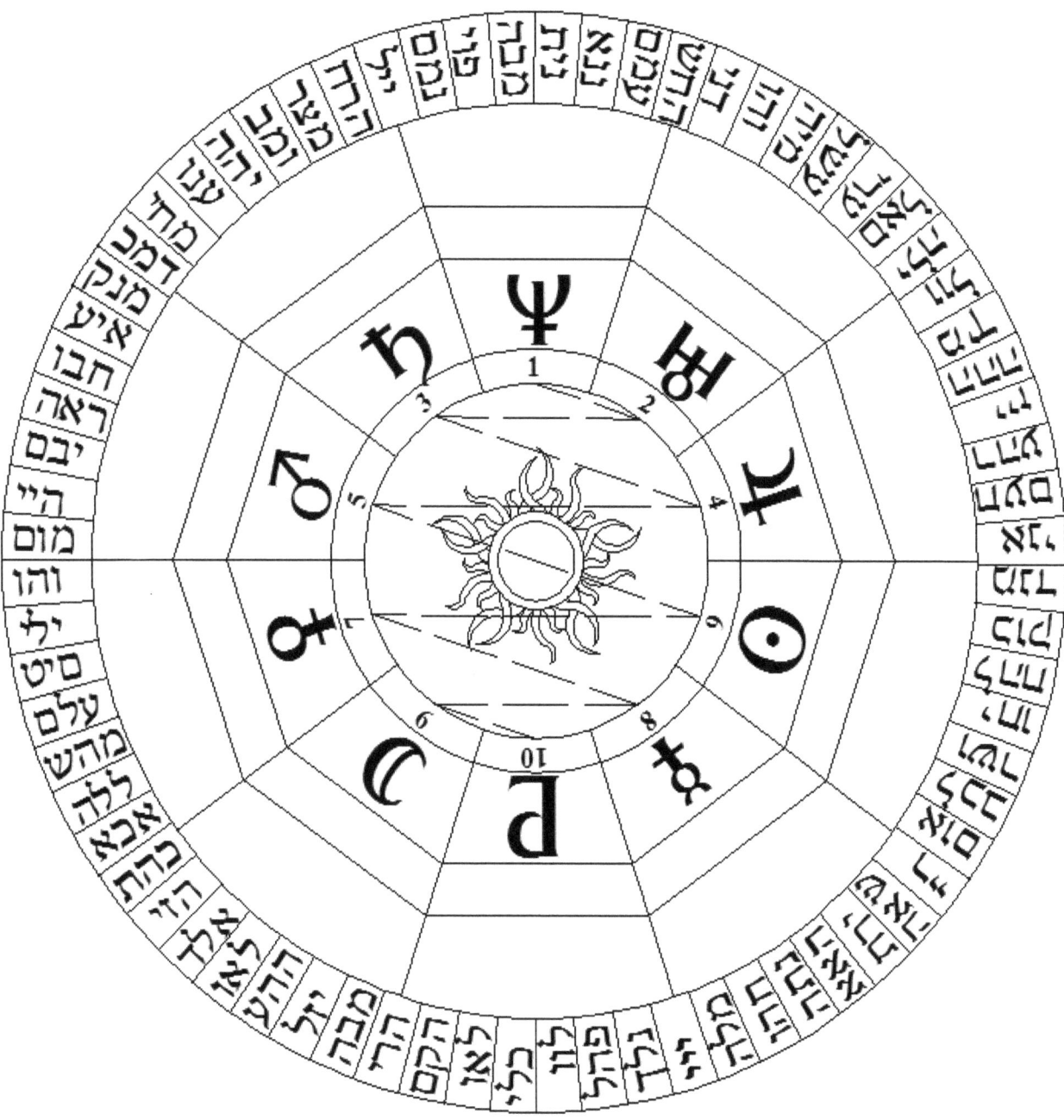

Legend:

Centre Sun	Owner of Amulet, at the centre of their universe.
Flash 1-10	Lightning flash symbolic of your journey into life to learn on earth.
1st circle	Numerical order of journey into the manifestation..
2nd circle	Order of Planets that rule over the stations on the tree of life.
3rd circle	Space to fill in the Names of your Guiding Lights
4th circle	Space for Hebrew letters of your Guiding Lights
5th circle	Energy of the 72 Guiding Lights all around you.

Appendix A
List of Guiding Lights

No.	Guiding Light	Symbol	Ruling Date	Ruling Degree
1	Vehu	והו	21 Mar - 25 Mar	Aries 0° - 4°
2	Yeli	ילי	26 Mar - 30 Mar	Aries 5° - 9°
3	Sit	סיט	31 Mar - 4 Apr	Aries 10° - 14°
4	Elem	עלם	5 Apr - 9 Apr	Aries 15° - 19°
5	Mahash	מהש	10 Apr - 14 Apr	Aries 20° - 24°
6	Lelah	ללה	15 Apr - 20 Apr	Aries 25° - 30°
7	Acha	אכא	21 Apr - 25 Apr	Taurus 0° - 4°
8	Kahet	כהת	26 Apr - 30 Apr	Taurus 5° - 9°
9	Hezi	הזי	1 May - 5 May	Taurus 10° - 14°
10	Elad	אלד	6 May - 10 May	Taurus 15° - 19°
11	Lav	לאו	11 May - 15 May	Taurus 20° - 24°
12	Haha	ההע	16 May - 20 May	Taurus 25° - 30°
13	Yezel	יזל	21 May - 25 May	Gemini 0° - 4°
14	Mebah	מבה	26 May - 31 May	Gemini 5° - 9°
15	Hari	הרי	1 Jun - 5 Jun	Gemini 10° - 14°
16	Hakem	הקם	6 Jun - 10 Jun	Gemini 15° - 19°
17	Lav	לאו	11 Jun - 16 Jun	Gemini 20° - 24°
18	Keli	כלי	17 Jun - 21 Jun	Gemini 25° - 30°
19	Lov	לוו	22 Jun - 26 Jun	Cancer 0° - 4°
20	Pahal	פהל	27 Jun - 1 Jul	Cancer 5° - 9°
21	Nelach	נלך	2 Jul - 6 Jul	Cancer 10° - 14°
22	Yeyay	ייי	7 Jul - 11 Jul	Cancer 15° - 19°

23	Melah	מלה	12 Jul - 16 Jul	Cancer 20° - 24°
24	Chaho	חהו	17 Jul - 22 Jul	Cancer 25° - 30°
25	Netah	נתה	23 Jul - 27 Jul	Leo 0° - 4°
26	Ha'a	האא	28 Jul - 1 Aug	Leo 5° - 9°
27	Yeret	ירת	2 Aug - 6 Aug	Leo 10° - 14°
28	Sha'ah	שאה	7 Aug - 14 Aug	Leo 15° - 19°
29	Riyi	ריי	13 Aug - 17 Aug	Leo 20° - 24°
30	Om	אום	18 Aug - 22 Aug	Leo 25° - 30°
31	Lekav	לכב	23 Aug - 28 Aug	Virgo 0° - 4°
32	Vesher	ושר	29 Aug - 2 Sep	Virgo 5° - 9°
33	Yichu	יחו	3 Sep - 7 Sep	Virgo 10° - 14°
34	L'hach	להח	8 Sep - 12 Sep	Virgo 15° - 19°
35	Kevek	בוק	13 Sept - 17 Sep	Virgo 20° - 24°
36	Menad	מנד	18 Sep - 23 Sep	Virgo 25° - 30°
37	Ani	אני	24 Sep - 28 Sep	Libra 0° - 4°
38	Cha'am	חעם	29 Sep - 3 Oct	Libra 5° - 9°
39	Reho	רהע	4 Oct - 8 Oct	Libra 10° - 14°
40	Yeyiz	ייז	9 Oct - 13 Oct	Libra 15° - 19°
41	Hahah	ההה	14 Oct - 18 Oct	Libra 20° - 24°
42	Mich	מיך	19 Oct - 23 Oct	Libra 25° - 30°
43	Veval	וול	24 Oct - 28 Oct	Scorpio 0° - 4°
44	Yelah	ילה	29 Oct - 2 Nov	Scorpio 5° - 9°
45	Se'al	סאל	3 Nov - 7 Nov	Scorpio 10° - 14°
46	Ari	ערי	8 Nov - 12 Nov	Scorpio 15° - 19°
47	Eshal	עשל	13 Nov - 17 Nov	Scorpio 20° - 24°
48	Mih	מיה	18 Nov - 22 Nov	Scorpio 25° - 30°

#	Name	Hebrew	Dates	Degrees
49	Vehu	והו	23 Nov - 27 Nov	Sagittarius 0° - 4°
50	Dani	דני	28 Nov - 2 Dec	Sagittarius 5° - 9°
51	Hachash	החש	3 Dec - 7 Dec	Sagittarius 10° - 14°
52	Omem	עמם	8 Dec - 12 Dec	Sagittarius 15° - 19°
53	Nena	ננא	13 Dec - 16 Dec	Sagittarius 20° - 24°
54	Nit	נית	17 Dec - 21 Dec	Sagittarius 25° - 30°
55	Mivah	מבה	22 Dec - 26 Dec	Capricorn 0° - 4°
56	Poi	פוי	27 Dec - 31 Dec	Capricorn 5° - 9°
57	Nemem	נמם	1 Jan - 5 Jan	Capricorn 10° - 14°
58	Yeyil	ייל	6 Jan - 10 Jan	Capricorn 15° - 19°
59	Harach	הרח	11 Jan - 15 Jan	Capricorn 20° - 24°
60	Metzer	מצר	16 Jan - 20 Jan	Capricorn 25° - 30°
61	Umab	ומב	21 Jan - 25 Jan	Aquarius 0° - 4°
62	Yahah	יהה	26 Jan - 30 Jan	Aquarius 5° - 9°
63	Anu	ענו	31 Jan - 4 Feb	Aquarius 10° - 14°
64	Machi	מחי	5 Feb - 9 Feb	Aquarius 15° - 19°
65	Dameb	דמב	10 Feb - 14 Feb	Aquarius 20° - 24°
66	Menak	מנק	15 Feb - 19 Feb	Aquarius 25° - 30°
67	Iya	איע	20 Feb - 24 Feb	Pisces 0° - 4°
68	Chavu	חבו	25 Feb - 29 Feb	Pisces 5° - 9°
69	Ra'ah	ראה	1 Mar - 5 Mar	Pisces 10° - 14°
70	Yabam	יבם	6 Mar - 10 Mar	Pisces 15° - 19°
71	Hayi	היי	11 Mar - 15 Mar	Pisces 20° - 24°
72	Mum	מום	16 Mar - 20 Mar	Pisces 25° - 30°

Bibliography

Books I found the inspiration from to create my colouring in learning book on the 72 Guiding Lights.

Jacobus G. Swart: *The Book of Self Creation.* The Sangreal Sodality Press 2009
--- *The Book of Sacred Names.* The Sangreal Sodality Press 2011
--- *The Book of Seals & Amulets.* The Sangreal Sodality Press 2014.

Piers A. Vaughan: trans. of *The Practical Kabbalah* by Robert Ambelain,

Charles E.O Carter: *The Principles of Astrology.* The Theosophical Publishing House, 1931

Margaret E. Hone: *The Modern Text-Book of Astrology* Redwood Books 1951

Yehuda Berg: *The Seventy-two Names of God "Technology for the Soul, Kabalah Centre* 2003

Sepharial: The New *Manual of Astrology in Four Books, William Rider & Son, LTD 1898*

www.ingramcontent.com/pod-product-compliance
Lightning Source LLC
Chambersburg PA
CBHW080247170426
43192CB00014BA/2594